Coping with Karma

Recognizing your life's path

Joop van Dam

Translated by Jakob M. Cornelius

Hawthorn Press
Stroud

Published by Hawthorn Press, Bankfield House,
13 Wallbridge, Stroud GL5 3JA, UK

British Library Cataloguing in Publication Data
Dam, Joop van
    Coping with karma: Recognizing your life's
    path. – (Biography and self-development series)
    I. Title II. Series
    133.58122

ISBN 1 869 890 33 7

Cover design by David Newbatt, Newton Dee
Typeset by Bookman Ltd, Bristol
Printed by Billings & Son Ltd, Worcester

Preface to
the English Translation

To read about karma and reincarnation in the comfort of one's home or in a study group is very different from applying it to one's own life-situation. It may seem to us that we are very far away from the direct experience of the laws of karma that Rudolf Steiner had, but Joop van Dam shows in this book that we are much closer to such experience than we may at first think. The path of knowledge given by Rudolf Steiner involves the practice of intimate soul exercises that not only prepare the student for spiritual experience but provide for a genuine soul hygiene which provides the best foundation for coping with our own life experiences – and also leads to insight into their source. In particular, Joop van Dam shows in detail how the retrospective review of the day, perhaps the most fundamental and far reaching of Steiner's exercises, leads to this, especially when coupled to the power of the night. Although we are not conscious of our experiences when deeply asleep, they have great importance for the day, particularly regarding the way we open ourselves to the future.

A deeply felt appreciation of karma gives us confidence in the future, for then we know that it brings us what we most need to grow spiritually, and in such a way that we may most readily benefit from it.

Nick Thomas

Author's Preface

The premise of this book is that man undergoes a process of development that is not confined to one life only; that in this developmental process other lives have preceded the current one, and more are to follow. In man's existence between death and a new birth, past deeds are evaluated and digested. At the same time the subsequent life on earth is prepared: circumstances are sought that allow for a meaningful sequel to what has been brought about earlier on. In this process, the human being receives the help of hierarchical beings active in the spiritual world.

In this sense, the destiny, or karma, the human being encounters on earth is something that has been purposely decided upon by his own higher being. But it has the character of an offer being made. How one responds is largely still a matter of one's own free choice. For example, at birth every human being receives a body in and by means of which he

will live his life. It is his 'house'. Every house
has its limitations, and, on the other hand,
its potential. How we live in our house is
up to us.

How to become aware of what the world has
to offer us in life is the subject of this booklet.

The text is an edited version of a talk given
at Whitsun, 1986.

J. van Dam

Contents

1. Introduction

> For one must gain insight into the deed,
> pay attention also to not doing.
> The essence of doing lies deeply con-
> cealed.
>
> (Fourth conversation of the charioteer
> with Arjuna in the *Bhagavad Gita*)

Any human life has moments that turn out to be key moments – those of which one can say 'A change in direction occurred here'. This change in direction may be an accident, or an illness with a lasting effect. Or it may be a turn of events that still leaves some options open – one can either revert to the previous course or stay on the new one. In both cases, however, it is a matter of a course being set.

In his autobiography, Laurens van der Post describes just such a key moment. Besides his books about Africa and the Bushmen, van der Post has also written – in *Night of the New Moon* and in his autobiography, *Yet Being Someone Other* – about the time he was a

1

prisoner of war in Indonesia in the Second World War. During this time he was able to do much to help his fellow prisoners because of his profound understanding of the psyche of the Japanese camp guards. When, during the war, his unit was surrounded by Japanese soldiers, he was able to save his own life and that of his comrades by calling out in Japanese, and in the most polite form (in the Japanese language there are several grades of politeness), that he had something to tell them. The Japanese lowered their guns, open-mouthed.

How had it come about that van der Post was able to do this? It had its origin in what he calls in his autobiography, *Yet Being Someone Other*, 'the incident of the two cups of coffee'. As a young man he was working as a journalist in Pretoria where his beat was the port. One day in the cafe he used to frequent he heard the owner call out to two customers entering, 'Hey, you! Out! I don't want you in here!' He went over, saw that the two people standing there were not European, and asked the owner 'Why are you doing this?' The owner said 'If I allow these coloureds in here, I'll lose my customers.' To which van der Post replied 'but if you don't, you'll lose my custom. Gentlemen, may I invite you for a cup of coffee?' And he led them to a quiet corner of the cafe. They turned out to be two Japanese journalists with whom, in the course of the next few days, he became closely acquainted. Two weeks later he received a dinner invitation from a brand-new Japanese ship lying in port – as a result of the intercession of his two Japanese colleagues, it turned out later. To make a long story short, he ended up joining the ship on a goodwill voyage for half a year, and stayed in Japan for several months, all the while immersing himself deeply in the Japanese language and folk-spirit.

The incident of the two cups of coffee was an opportunity for initiative, which became pivotal in determining the course of his further life (and, later on, even that of others). It was like deliberately throwing a switch, the results of which became evident only much later.

Such obvious moments,which stand out like beacons, are rare. Most of the time it takes more effort to kindle an awareness of destiny.

For a start, it is necessary to look back on one's own life, as van der Post does in his autobiography. We can look back on our own lives in several different ways. A few variations of such a *retrospect* will be discussed next.

2. The Retrospect

A. The effects of a retrospect

Many people experience periods in their lives when they feel rudderless. Nothing happens to the. They would like to 'have a go' at something, but do not know what. So they grope in the dark. Life no longer makes sense.

In such situations, a retrospect exercise has been shown to be especially effective. What this involves it to look back on the events of the day for four or five minutes each evening. In order to gain a certain focus, one asks a specific question which acts like a window offering a certain view. For instance 'What was the most significant encounter I had today?' This does not always have to have been an encounter with another person; it may also be a new dish one has tasted for the first time, having seen a budding leaf in spring, or having noticed the light of the evening sun on the landscape. This experience is recalled for a few moments; one allows it to light up in the illunination of one's consciousness. One

then makes a brief note of it. The latter is
an essential part of the exercise as it ensures
that the act of recalling is made concrete. It is
like signing a report to oneself. And if there
has been no encounter, this is also noted –
'Nothing'. But it will soon be noticed that this
happens less and less.

After a few weeks the 'window' is changed.
Another question is asked, for instance 'What
was the miracle of the day?' This may be
something that unexpectedly turned out differ-
ently from what had been anticipated, and yet
became a decisive factor. Or 'Which questions
were I asked today?' Gradually it becomes
apparent that one does have all kinds of experiences; that something is happening inwardly,
that one is not as empty inside as it seemed.
And then the will awakens again, be it at first
in a general way – much like the way it is in
spring, when the earth starts to turn green
with the appearance of new leaves, which,
by and large, look much alike. But as one
persists in this daily inner activity, one's
own individual will begins to appear, just as
the simple form of the first leaves turns into
the more differentiated forms of subsequent
leaves. It becomes possible once again to live
creatively, to respond actively to the opportu-
nities that offer themselves in life. Later on we
shall return to this experience of looking back

consciously on the *past* and thereby rousing the will for the *future*.

B. The retrospect as an exercise

Rudolf Steiner gave many indications on the subject of pursuing a path of inner development in daily life. The retrospect constitutes an indispensable and irreplaceable element of this path. In that context, however, the exercise has a different character, a different purpose from what has been described so far. Whereas in the activity described earlier the subjective element came to the fore (deepening the experiences one has had), the retrospect when done as part of a path of inner development emphasizes objectivity.

There are two ways in which this objectivity can be practised, each resulting in a different kind of retrospect. They are described in separate places. In one form of retrospect, described in Steiner's book *Occult Science: An Outline*, the events of the day are recalled as exactly as possible, but in reverse order – from the end of the day back to the beginning. The emphasis is on *observation*, as exact and in as much detail as possible.

The other retrospect is described in another of Rudolf Steiner's basic books, *Knowledge of the Higher Worlds: How is it Achieved?* Here, objectivity is brought into it by learning to differentiate between the essential and the non-essential. The emphasis is on *judgement*, learning to evaluate (to assess validity, one could also say).

It is this second form that is especially difficult. To relive the sentiments of the moment is usually a poor standard by which to judge because it draws one into the event once again. Steiner's advice is to assess the situation as if one were a spectator – as if the event concerned not oneself, but a stranger. One should not, in a manner of speaking, be part of the event. Only then may it become clear what was truly essential and what was not.

In both types of retrospect one gets an inkling of one's destiny. The judgemental form highlights the key moments of the day, or of a longer time-span. The further back in the past an occurrence lies, the more one can distance oneself from it and the clearer its objective significance becomes. But the form of retrospect in which the emphasis is on observation also awakens in us a sense of how destiny plays into our lives.

Destiny arises out of our encounters with the world. The environment one is born into, and in which one lives, is of decisive signifi cance. This includes the ethnic environ ment, country, parents, type of society, educational system, etc. In the interaction with these factors, one's personality is formed and developed.

An important aspect of the 'environment' in which we live is our own bodily nature. Whether one is tall or short, near- or farsighted, inclined to be overweight or thin, normally healthy or handicapped in some way – all of these conditions are part of the circumstances our inner being is confronted with. In fact, subconsciously we seek this confrontation, for we have ourselves chosen the circumstances.

This view, namely that of one's bodily nature being an expression of one's destiny, has a part to play not only in the individual path of development but also in the relationships one has with other people. When someone has professional relations with other people, for instance as a teacher or a therapist, an awareness of the reality of destiny gives a new dimension to one's work. The realization that someone's physical constitution, with its positive as well as its problematic sides, truly belongs to that person as a self-imposed task has the effect that one can accept this person in a new way – not in the sense of accepting the condition, but of helping the person to overcome the obstacle and thereby to develop

new capacities. The preparation for this lies in
the objective observation of the other's bodily
instrument, in attention to details such as the
shape of the hands, the posture, the sound
of the voice, the colour of the eyes, etc. In
short, a 'physiognomical observation' of the
bodily phenomena of the other human being.
When one makes an attempt to experience this
constitution inwardly oneself, one may get an
inkling of the potential and of the obstacles
inherent in it. Often this has the result that
one gets an initial intuition of how a certain
one-sidedness or weakness may be overcome
or how a certain advantage may be exploited.

The observation of external phenomena has
an objectifying effect. And, indeed, with each
subsequent meeting erroneous impressions or
memory-images may be corrected.

C. Karma research

Towards the end of his life, Steiner gave many
lectures about reincarnation and karma. He
dealt with this subject from numerous different points of view in an attempt to make it
accessible and acceptable to twentieth-century
consciousness. Thereby he actually laid the
foundation for a new kind of social awareness.

In the course of these lectures Steiner indicated how he arrived at the results of his spiritual-scientific research, and how others, too, can come to these results. To be sure, his method makes high demands on those who wish to carry out this kind of research. And a characteristic feature is that the first step consists of looking back on specific life situations, and that this retrospect has a definite 'physiognomical' character. This type of investigation can then lead to an insight into situations from previous lives.

It would be beyond the scope of the present discussion to describe these methods of research here. One may read about them in the right context in the relevant printed lectures by Rudolf Steiner, for instance in the lecture of 9 May 1924 (published in *Karmic Relations, Vol. II*) and also in a number of lectures of 1912 published under the title *Reincarnation and Karma*.

The exercises discussed here have the effect of awakening an awareness of destiny in a more general sense.

D. Retrospective exercises for social life

In a lecture printed under the English title *Social and Antisocial Forces in Man*, Steiner recommends two exercises that, although they have a different main purpose, are at the same time highly effective in raising one's awareness of one's destiny.

Both exercises are intended to stimulate and develop social impulses the human being does not possess naturally in modern times. Each of these exercises involves a form of retrospect, although in this case covering not just a single day but a much longer period in one's life.

I start with the second exercise. One looks back on events in one's own life in the way described in *Knowledge of the Higher Worlds: How is it Achieved?* One looks at oneself as one was earlier on, in the way we have called 'judgemental', attempting to distinguish the essential from the non-essential. The past experience is not relived as such, but one evaluates what *really* occurred. Then the way the past event was actually experienced begins to lose its significance.

Our 'I', says Steiner, is encapsulated in its experiences – not only those of the present, but also those of the past. These experiences always tend to colour our view of the world. This encapsulated 'I', formed out of the experiences of the past, is an accumulation of egoism, for the world is continually experienced in direct relation to the self. The idea now is to peel off the earlier experiences. When this is achieved – and what makes this possible is the distinguishing of the essential from the non-essential, as the observer of oneself – one's outlook on the world becomes free again. The human being is set free from his imprisonment by his experiences; he becomes open-minded. And this is a social force in our relations with other people.

The other exercise, the first, has the character of exact observation. With respect to this exercise, Steiner advised that instead of looking at yourself as the centre of events you should look at the periphery, at the people around you. These may be your parents, your teachers, your friends and, indeed, your enemies; these are all people that have presented you with challenges of some sort and have thus had a part in forming you. For the larger part, you are what you are now thanks to the encounters with these other people. Just try to recall one or more of these people, as they were in these part encounters, as exactly as you can – where they were standing, how they spoke, what they did, as clearly as possible, with an eye for details. Then go to an earlier situation, another image, etc. After a while you may have the experience that the images you are creating become so vivid that they make 'gestures' you recognize but did not remember. What this brings about is a picture of the other that is free of sympathy or antipathy – an objective picture without love or hate.

If you are successful in this with people you have known in the past, it also becomes a capacity with respect to people you meet in the present. You learn to see them in a way in which sympathy or antipathy play no part, whether you like them or not. This, said Steiner (less than a year before the first Waldorf School was founded), would also be of the greatest importance in pedagogy. For as a result of this capacity to form an objective picture of the people around us, a new social force is engendered in us. The first exercise brings about *open-mindedness*, the second *gratitude* (one may also say *positivity*).

The question is 'Where do these social impulses come from?' Rudolf Steiner's answer, at first glance, is astonishing – they come from the night.

3. The Night

In ordinary daily life, twentieth-century man, in as far as he asserts himself as an ego being, is antisocial. There is no getting around this. Each time his ego-consciousnes enters a new phase – for the first time at age 3, then again at age 9, and so on – he says 'no' to the world, he is antisocial. And this is necessary in order for him to develop a consciousness of self. As human beings, we are social as a matter of course only during the night. In as far as we are social during the day, it is due to the influence of the impulses of the night extending into the day.

One could turn this insight into a kind of motto, a practical guideline: I can become social in as far as I can succeed in allowing the influences of the night to work through into my day. The question is 'How do I do this?' We already know the answer. The social forces working out of the night into the day are activated by the retrospect.

When you have a problem with someone – when something seems to go wrong each time you meet, when something always gets in the way and inwardly you always seem to respond negatively to this person, and so on – experience shows that it can be beneficial when, for a few consecutive evenings, you try to evoke images of this person with the kind of exactness described earlier. What is the colour of his/her eyes? What is the shape of the forehead? How does he/she walk? What do their hands look like when at rest? And so on. Then the next time you get together you notice there is a difference. Something has happened, and obviously it has happened in the intervening nights.

A retrospect is usually done in the evening. In essence it is a preparation for the night. This is comparable to adjusting the compass and hoisting the sails; you sail into the night with a clear destination. And something takes place during the night What takes place is something we shall return to later.

On waking in the morning, you forget everything that took place during the night. It is no longer in your consciousness. We do not by nature retain our consciousness of the night. One purpose of a path of self development is to regain the ability to remain conscious of night experiences, but we have not yet progressed that far.

And yet, whatever has taken place during the night is not lost. We hold on to it somewhere else in our being. During the night our higher being has been able to work, to observe, to experience, and it is changed as it digests the experiences of the previous day. The higher 'I' is the core of our being. It is active there where we are most truly ourselves, but at the same time it works where our day-consciousness penetrates least, namely in our will. It is only very gradually that we become aware in the course of our lives of what it really is that we want to do in life. The will is always there, but latent, hidden. In the morning we notice that what took place during the night becomes active in our will. It affects the manner in which the will is directed at the world. It becomes apparent that a kind of reversal has taken place in our awareness of destiny, that there is a change in direction.

When we speak of our awareness of destiny we have to realize that this awareness can take two directions. In the first place, what we associate with destiny is, of course, the *past*. Certain occurrences take place because in an earlier life we did certain things that necessitate these subsequent occurrences. Someone has a given bodily constitution or a certain disposition due to earlier deeds, etc. This past-oriented aspect of destiny always has the inherent danger of appearing as a Calvinistic shadow of predestination that seems to hang over us. The inexorability of this 'law of Moses' may also add a restrictive one-sidedness and a potentially paralysing element.

Still, this look into the past is necessary. The exercises we have spoken of so far consist of an exact observation of what occurred in the past. And with this retrospect we enter the night. What then takes place is a number of intensive digestive processes. And in the morning something, apparently, has changed. The impulses that are awakened in us do not lie in the imaginative, awake memories directed inward, but in an anticipatory will directed at the world. As already said, a reversal took place. One could express it thus – destiny does not lie behind, in the past, but *ahead*; it approaches us from the world of the *future*.

In the changed consciousness of the morning the beginning of a new dawn announces itself. But what exactly occurs during the night?

Rudolf Steiner discussed this in a lecture given in Breslau on 14 June 1924 (published in *Karmic Relations Vol. VII*). He first drew attention to the difference between the experience of going to sleep and that of awakening. Going to sleep usually involves a positive sense of wellbeing. The events of the day become ever more vague and less of a burden. They are abandoned, as it were. One becomes lighter and this produces a positive mood. Waking up is quite different. Unless one is drawn immediately into the sense impressions of sound, light and colour, one may have something like a feeling of heaviness, as if one has come up out of the depths, carrying a burden which is now dragged into the day. As the day wears on, one is gradually relieved of this burden – it wears off. What is the cause of this feeling?

Steiner described how during sleep the spirit-soul of the human being traverses a kind of loop. At night, when going to sleep, it departs from the living body, but it does this in a particular way: it moves out via the head. It becomes larger and larger, goes around in a circuit, and in the morning, during awakening, it re-enters via the limbs, 'via the fingers and the toes'. These are two entirely different processes, constitutionally different one might say – one pertaining to the morning and the other to the evening. In the course of the day the spirit-soul being moves from the limbs to the head. For some this path is traversed quickly – these are the morning people. For others it takes more time – these are the evening people who do not become productive until nighttime.

In the morning you still bear within you something of the experiences of the night. These night experiences, Steiner declared, are comparable, to some extent, to the soul experiences of the day, which consist of two aspects. One aspect involves the thoughts and feelings evoked by the various impressions of life. But mixed in with this aspect is that which rises up within us as memories of the past.

Our night experiences similarly consist of two 'streams'. One originates in falling asleep and the other is centered on awakening. The experience-stream originating in falling asleep is comparable to the experiences of the first decades after death, when each human being relives the experiences of their past life, but from a different standpoint – each person experiences as a reality their entire life's daytime activity but in the exact way those who felt the effects of one's deeds experienced them, physically as well as morally. At night one experiences something similar in the stream originating in falling asleep, but in this instance it only takes the form of images instead of the reality one experiences after death in preparation for a newly emerging karma. This night experience is like the experience of daily events via the senses.

But there is also a second stream, which is comparable to memory in day-consciousness. This stream has the character of something gigantic, something 'enormous' in format. This is what you experience on awakening, and the impression keeps tugging at you for part of the day. What lives in this second stream is one's life destiny. In each period of sleep, one's entire karmic past passes in review before the soul. Just as in the process of going to sleep the human being gets a foretaste of new karma being formed for future earth lives, so, upon awakening, he senses the karma he has already formed, the karma in effect at present. Just as in day-consciousness we have the memories of past events alongside the experiences of the moment, so, during the night, we have the memories of previous earth lives beside the experience of the past day's events. Soon upon falling asleep the latest of our previous lives passes in review, then the next previous, and so on. Thus, the night is a window through which the human being views his karma.

An entirely new and different light is thrown on the significance of sleep when we realize that each night we submerge ourselves in sleep in order to work on the shaping of our future destiny (first stream), and that between going to sleep and waking up the impulse is given by one's past karma to take action in daily life. Out of the second stream we carry something with us into the day. From out of the night, destiny reaches into daily life.

In the case of profoundly significant events —

those that are of a decisive nature with respect to destiny – one may have some awareness of the influence of the night. One is seized by a kind of unrest, by an inexplicable tension which may even be noticeable physically, until the totally unexpected event that was actually in store all along takes place and the tension is relieved. From the moment of awakening, which in such a case you experience as being different itself, you lived towards the decisive moment, as it were.

In the past this kind of experience was much more common. Almost everyone was familiar with it. This is why people disliked being woken from sleep suddenly; the intimate experiences that awakening can give are torn away, are overwhelmed by such rude awakenings. The farmer, said Steiner, did not immediately look out the window upon awakening, but kept his eyes averted in order to remain in darkness for a few moments longer while he could perceive what sleep yielded to the day. He liked to wake up slowly, with the distant singing of the birds and the pealing of the church bells. This allowed him to prepare for the moment of transition from night to day. Thus, in the light of the dawn he had a premonition, a sense, of what destiny had in store for him in the course of the day.

Destiny is related to the will. Our legs carry

us wherever we need to go in order to meet that part of our destiny that is still waiting for us out in the world. From the point of view of our bodily constitution, this unprejudiced will lives in us most strongly during the morning hours. This, after all, is when our soul-spirit being enters our body, via the limbs. The morning is world oriented, action oriented. That is when we have the vitality to confront the world, to face whatever comes our way.

The morning is always young, full of hope, and future oriented. In the early morning even an industrial city may look beautiful, with the sun rising and people gradually taking up their tasks. Shortly after waking up you can still see everything without prejudice, without too many impressions getting in the way. As the day wears on your conceptions and observations take on more and more importance. They carry more weight than at the beginning of the day. In the morning you are much more capable of unprejudiced, open-minded action than you are in the afternoon or evening.

When our will is fresh, it is able to penetrate deeply into the world, and to face whatever is waiting for it there. A beautiful image of this is to be found in the Brothers Grimm's fairy tale of *The Drummer*. In this fairy tale, day and night experiences alternate continually. The hero of this tale goes into the forest in the early morning. This forest, so he has been told by the princess he wants to save, is full of giants. But nothing happens. He then beats a roll on his drum, causing the birds to fall from the trees. 'That will wake them up, those lazy-bones' he says. This is fresh will, full of enthusiasm for what comes.

This fresh strength of soul must be guarded, however. Someone once told me 'The ideas that come to me when I am shaving in the morning are often the best of the day. They are the ones to take note of.' Many people have the experience that 'the morning is wiser than the evening', according to a Russian proverb. That is why it makes a difference whether you wake up by yourself or with the alarm clock, whether you still have time to muse dreamily and catch whatever comes out of sleep and can take it with you as the mood for the coming day.

4. Being Open to the Future

There are certain moods of soul that may be practised to enable one to enter the day with a listening, receptive attitude. This kind of inner orientation protects the open-minded, unprejudiced will, prepared to meet whatever approaches out of the world as karma.

The first exercise is to acquire *a sense of union with the world*. We are connected with the world around us in a mysterious way. Rudolf Steiner pointed this out by referring to the peculiar phenomenon whereby criminals so often have an irresistable urge to return to the scene of their crime. This, in fact, is a general human trait. We retain a connection with what we have done, with the circumstances of our deeds. These connections are like invisible threads. This is where the destiny that lies behind us is clear-cut. In the morning, however, this is turned around. That is when we

25

experience the connections with the world that are still awaiting us. Although they are still approaching, we nevertheless already have a tie with them. It is the destiny in front of us. This will be an inborn, human soul mood only in the future. But we can already work on it. In the book *Knowledge of the Higher Worlds: How is it Achieved?* this soul mood is described as one of the prerequisites for inner development; to feel part of the whole. Steiner gives two examples. As an educator, when a pupil does not meet your expectations you should not look for the cause in the child, but in yourself: 'Isn't what he lacks the result of how I act?' In the case of a criminal one may, in a similar sense, have the thought 'Perhaps he has become what he is because the very care once lavished on me was denied him.' An extension of this attitude is the idea that you are a link in the totality, and consequently co-responsible for everything that happens.

What kind of law is this that joins one part to others to make a whole? It is the law of life forces. The world of life always creates totalities. This is why our own life force is a healing force. When one part goes out of joint, the result is illness. When it is restored to its proper function, the whole organism becomes healthy again. A sense of unison with the world teaches us that we form part of a living tissue in the world, that everything we do has its consequences in the world and that it returns to us.

The second soul mood that may be acquired by practice is *thankfulness*. Steiner mentioned this in his lecture of 14 June 1924 referred to earlier. From thankfulness, he said, love is born, and love opens the heart to the forces of spirit penetrating life. This feeling of thankfulness is naturally present in every human being underneath the threshold of consciousness. It is part of night-man. Even if someone does something terrible to you, and in your ordinary consciousness you are deeply hurt, thankfulness still lives in the depths of the soul, for everything we undergo enriches us. Even the most difficult experiences that befall us have something to bestow on us, even though it may not be so easy to discern it.

A beautiful example of consciously experienced thankfulness is found in Jacob's battle with the angel. Jacob exclaims 'I won't let go of you until you have blessed me.'

A third soul mood that can be practised, which lies close to thankfulness, is *trust in life*. Trust is a capacity man is born with. It is evident in every young child. It is hard to imagine it being otherwise. Each child entering the world radiates trust like a shining beacon, which cannot but find response from fellow human beings. A very small child's trust is generally not betrayed. But then, gradually, the radiance of the world behind the portal of birth diminishes, not only for the child itself but perceptible also to those around it. At the same time the innate force of trust which enveloped the child also fades. The first metamorphosis takes place: the child learns to have self-confidence. It becomes aware that it can function and develop in this world as an independent being, and is no longer entirely dependent on the world. Innate trust becomes self-confidence.

Only then does the third step in the development of trust become possible. The human being becomes aware that his development does not depend only on himself, but it is life itself that makes growth possible. And, once again, trust is metamorphosed, and now becomes trust in life, trust in destiny. This means trusting that whatever befalls you, whatever you have to go through, embodies the potential for development. This is not a waiting attitude, but an inwardly active one which comes to expression in the deed. Characteristic of this kind of trust is the drummer boy of the Grimm's fairy tale.

This force also underlies the statement attributed to (the Dutch stadtholder) William of Orange: 'One need not guarantee results in order to undertake something.'

Just as trust in life goes with thankfulness, so is there something to be added to the first soul mood mentioned, that of a sense of union with the world, and this is a striving to *remain open-minded in one's relationship to the world* i.e. to keep free from prejudice with respect to whatever happens.

The well known psychologist Abraham Maslow calls this force 'the continual freshness of appreciation'. Art historian Herbert Read calls it 'the innocent eye of the child'. Toward the end of the 1960s, a popular saying proclaimed 'This is the *first* day of the rest of your life'. A French version of this idea, much older in origin, says it even better: 'Plein de courage, plein d'amour, plein d'espoir pour la vie, que Dieu me donnera' – 'Full of courage, love and hope for the life God has in store for me'. The forces of hope and renewal are the fresh, young soul forces related to the will and to the morning.

A sense of being part of the whole, thankfulness, trust, and staying open-minded in one's relation to the world – these are the inner moods by means of which the soul opens itself to the destiny approaching it out of the world. They bring about a sunrise in the soul itself. Because of this inner sun, the world appears in a new light.

5. Living with the Influences of Morning and Evening

Rudolf Steiner often wrote down the results of his spiritual research in brief sentences. Two sentences from his notebook pertaining to the aforementioned lecture of 14 June 1924 are cited here in the way of a summary and conclusion.

The first sentence is as follows: 'The thoughts of morning illuminate karma' (*'Morgengedanken, sie erhellen das Karma'*). The consciousness connected with the morning allows karma to light up, as it were. Upon awakening, when inwardly turning towards the realm of the night, listening, one can allow the spirit light of the night to shine and thus gain an awareness of one's destiny.

Immediately following is the second sentence: 'The thoughts of evening must prepare the illumination' (*'Abendgedanken, sie sollen*

die Erhellung vorbereiten'). In the morning the
light only shines when in the evening we have
worked for it; when, in a manner of speaking,
we ourselves have lit the flame with which we
enter the night. This light is the retrospect.

We have seen how there are many possibil-
ities: the intensive review of the day, but
also the review in which images are created
of oneself or others over a longer period of
time. With this conscious inward effort, with
these evening thoughts, we enter the realm of
the night.

During the night we are like an open book
to one another. This is where, so to say, 'the
book of karma' lies open for us. And this is also
where our social forces are alive, where they
are nourished, where they grow, on account of
the beholding of karma.

When the preparation in the evening has
been vigorous, one will, the next morning,
notice the fructifying effect of the night: it
is noticeable in one's sense of union with the
world, in thankfulness and trust, and in the
fresh willpower that, full of hope, engages
itself with the new day.

An actual awareness of our destiny takes
place in the night. It is our task to bring this
'night-consciousness into the day. The night
has two portals – that of falling asleep in the
evening and that of awakening in the morning.

Our waking consciousness can stand guard at these portals. In this sense one can say 'To work on one's awareness of one's destiny one begins by living with the forces of evening and morning.'

Bibliography

Grimm Brothers (Jakob and Wilhelm) (Editors), *Complete Grimm's Fairy Tales, The*, Routledge & Kegan Paul, London; 1975
———— *Grimm's Tales for Young and Old – The Complete Stories*, Victor Gollancz Ltd, London; 1978
Steiner, Rudolf, *Karmic Relations Vol. II*, Rudolf Steiner Press, London; 1974
———— *Karmic Relations Vol. VII*, Rudolf Steiner Press, London; 1973
———— *Knowledge of the Higher Worlds: How is it Achieved?*, Rudolf Steiner Press, London; 1989
———— *Occult Science: An Outline*, Rudolf Steiner Press, London; 1979
———— *Reincarnation and Karma: Their Significance in Modern Culture*, Anthroposophic Press, New York; 1985
———— *Social and Antisocial Forces in Man*, Mercury Press, New York; 1982
van der Post, Laurens, *Night of the New Moon*, Chatto, London; 1985
———— *Yet Being Someone Other*, Penguin Books, Harmondsworth; 1984

Also published by Hawthorn Press

How to Transform Thinking, Feeling and Willing

Jorgen Smit

The purpose of this book is clearly explained in the sub-title –
*Practical exercises for the training of thinking, feeling, willing,
imagination, composure, intuition, positivity and wonder*. Medi-
tation must be something that is wholly clear in the modern sense
of the word and the author enables readers to follow a modern-day
meditative path leading to deepened insight and awareness.

ISBN 1 869 890 17 5   217 mm x 138 mm; 64 pages
Social Ecology Series   Paperback

Life Patterns

Responding to life's questions, crises and challenges

Jerry Schottelndreier

Life Patterns offers a process, a method, that enables the reader to
take stock of their life situation – to gain an insight into their own
"setting" from a practical and spiritual point of view and to plan
the next steps to take.

ISBN 1 869 890 27 2   217 mm x 138 mm; 64 pages
Biography and Self-development Series   Paperback

Also published by Hawthorn Press

Man on the Threshold
The challenge of inner development

Bernard C.J. Lievegoed

Humanity is crossing a major threshold. The boundaries that have surrounded consciousness for centuries are becoming progressively less fixed and it is not only the physical world which now implies reality. Beyond this threshold the distinction between inner and outer experience no longer holds, and the experience of this can be extremely powerful – leading in some cases to psychological disturbances and illness, but for many bringing enlightenment and new insights which can induce them to change their priorities.

The theme of *Man on the Threshold* is the inner development and preparation required to rightly meet this all-embracing change of consciousness that is already upon us. Ancient and alternative paths of self-development are described – Egyptian, the Northern initiation mysteries, the medieval Christian approach, Eastern ways, the Rosicrucian stream – leading to the practical method of inner training and development needed today. The influence of the human double is examined, and the relationship between the human being, the earth and the planets, along with their medical and social implications.

ISBN 0 950 706 26 4   217 mm x 138 mm; 224 pages
Social Ecology Series   Paperback

Also published by Hawthorn Press

Rudolf Steiner
Life, work, inner path and social initiatives

Rudi Lissau

> *A very lucid, warm hearted and judicious ac-*
> *count of anthroposophy which I read with pleas-*
> *ure and gratitude.*

Saul Bellow
Nobel Prize winner

This book gives a vivid picture of Rudolf Steiner's life and work written in a very readable form. It highlights the relevance of Steiner's activities to contemporary social and human concerns and includes personal recollections of many people who met him or worked with him.

There are chapters on Steiner's philosophy; the universe, the earth and the human being; Christ and human destiny; the meditative path; education, social development, agriculture, science and art; and approaches to Steiner's work.

The author taught adolescents for over forty years at a Waldorf School based on the educational principles propounded by Rudolf Steiner. He has written and lectured widely on Steiner's work and philosophy.

ISBN 1 869 890 06 X   216 mm x 138 mm; 192 pages
Social Ecology Series   Paperback

If you have difficulties ordering from a bookshop, you can order direct from Hawthorn Press, Bankfield House, 13 Wallbridge, Stroud GL5 3JA, UK.

Telephone (0453) 757040   Fax (0453) 753295